MALALA YOUSAFZAI

THE GIRL WHO STOOD UP AGAINST THE TALIBAN

Biography for Kids 9-12

Children's Biography Books

BABY PROFESSOR
EDUCATION KIDS

Speedy Publishing LLC

40 E. Main St. #1156

Newark, DE 19711

www.speedypublishing.com

Copyright 2017

Malala Yousafzai is a Human Rights Activist who is best known for her fight for the rights of women in Pakistan to receive an education. In this book, we will be learning about her life and her accomplishments.

WHERE WAS MALALA YOUSAFZAI RAISED?

Malala was born on July 12, 1997 in the Swat Valley region of Pakistan. She was named after the famous Afghani warrior and poet Malalai of Maiwand.

MALALA YOUSAFZAI

PASHTUNS

S he was raised with her two younger brothers in the city of Mingora, Pakistan. As a family, they practiced the Islam religion and were part of the ethnic group that were known as the Pashtuns.

SCHOOLS

Her early childhood was one of peace and happiness. Her father ran several schools and was a teacher. Most Pakistani girls did not go to school; however, Malala did attend school at a school for girls that her father ran.

YOUNG PAKISTANI FEMALE STUDENTS

Girls in school in Khyber Pakhtunkhwa, Pakistan

She loved attending school and learning new things. She even dreamt about becoming a doctor, a politician or a teacher one day. She was an intelligent girl and learned three languages that included English, Pashto and Urdu. She was always encouraged by her father to learn more and he taught her that she would be able to accomplish anything that she desired.

THE TALIBAN TAKE CONTROL

When Malala was about ten years old, the Taliban started to take control over the region where she lived. They were very strict Muslims that demanded that everyone follow the law of the Islamic Sharia, and the women were told to stay home. When a woman left the home, she had to wear a burqa (which is clothing that covers her face, head and body), and she must be in the company of a male relative.

PROTEST RALLY AGAINST
Taliban

SHUTTING DOWN OF THE GIRLS SCHOOLS

As the Taliban continued to gain additional control, they also started enforcing new laws. These new laws included: women would not be permitted to have job or vote and music, movies, television, and dancing were not permitted. The Taliban eventually demanded that all of the girls' schools were to be shut down. If they were not shut down, they would be burned or destroyed.

THE BLOG

It was during this time period that the BBC approached Makala's father to find a female student that would write about life under control of the Taliban. Even though he was concerned about his family's safety, her father agreed that Malala could write the blog for the BBC, and it was named Diary of a Pakistani Schoolgirl. She wrote under her pen name, "Gul Makai", who was a Pashtun folktale heroine.

Malala Yousafzai speaks to the Department for International Development staff

S oon, Malala became known for the writings of her blog and started speaking in public regarding the treatment by the Taliban. The war then broke out in the Swat region when

the Pakistani government started fighting back against the Taliban. The government eventually took control back of this area and Malala was then able to return to school.

BEING SHOT

The Taliban were unhappy with Malala and her actions. The fighting had come to an end and schools were open once again, the Taliban remained throughout the city and Malala was instructed to discontinue speaking out and she also received many death threats.

SCHOOLS WERE OPEN AGAIN

On October 9, 2012, after school, she was taking the bus to her home when all of a sudden, a man that had a gun boarded the bus and asked, "Who is Malala?". He advised that he would kill them if they did not tell him who she was and he then proceeded to shoot Malala.

MALALA'S RECOVERY

Malala was struck in the head by the bullet and was very ill. She became conscious in the hospital a week later in England and the doctors were not sure whether she would live or if she had any brain damage. She needed a number of surgeries, but six months later she started to attend school once again.

MALALA YOUSAFZAI ON THE NEED FOR EDUCATION AT THE SUPPORTING SYRIA AND THE REGION

CONTINUING HER WORK

The bullet and her injuries did not stop Malala. She gave a speech on her 16th birthday to the United Nations. During this speech, she talked about her desire that all girls be able to get an education. Malala did not want violence or revenge on the Taliban, even for the man that shot her, she wanted just opportunity and peace for everyone.

Her impact and fame continues to grow and she has received several awards that include being a co-recipient of the 2014 Nobel Peace Prize. She was the youngest to ever receive this grand award. She shared the Nobel Peace Prize with Kailash Satyarthi who fought against slavery and child labor in India. She has also written a best-selling book titled I Am Malala.

WHAT IS ISLAM?

Islam is the religion that was founded by the Prophet Muhammad in the early 7th century. Islam followers believe in one god named Allah. The Quran is the primary Islam religious book.

WHAT IS THE DIFFERENCE BETWEEN ISLAM AND MUSLIM?

A person who follows and believes in the religion of Islam is a Muslim.

PORTRAIT OF THE PROPHET MUHAMMAD
RIDING THE BURAQ STEED

MUHAMMAD

Muhammad is known as the Holy Prophet of Islam and is the last prophet sent by Allah to mankind. He was born 570 CE and died 632 CE.

THE QURAN

Islam's sacred holy book is the Quran. Muslims believe the words of it were sent to Muhammad from Allah by an angel named Gabriel. Generally, in the Muslim home, the Quran is provided with a high place and sometimes there is a special stand that it is placed upon. No items are to be placed on top of a Quran. Abraham and Moses from the Christian Bible and the Jewish Torah also appear in Quran stories.

THE FIVE PILLARS OF ISLAM

The Five Pillars of Islam are five basic acts forming the framework of the Islam religion:

Shahadah: Shahadah is the basic declaration of faith, or creed, that a Muslim recites every time they pray. The translation in English is "There is no god, but God; Muhammad is the messenger of God."

Salat or Prayer: These prayers are said five times every day. As a Muslim is reciting these prayers, they must face to the holy city of Mecca. Typically, they go through certain motions and positions, using a prayer mat, while they are praying.

Zakat: This is giving of alms to the poor. Those which are able to afford it, have to give to the needy and poor

Hajj: This is known as the pilgrimage to Mecca. Each Muslim that is able to travel, and has funds for the trip, is to travel to Mecca at least one time during their life.

Fasting: During Ramadan, Muslims are required to fast (not drink or eat) between dawn and sunset. This ritual is intended to bring a believer closer to Allah. Not all Islamic followers are required to fast during this time. Those excused might include young people, sick people and pregnant women.

THE HADITH

Additional texts describing the sayings and actions of Muhammad which are not recorded in the Quran are known as the hadith. Typically, they were gathered by Islamic scholars following the death of Muhammad.

MOSQUES

A place of worship for followers of the Islam religion is called a mosque. Typically, there is a big prayer room where the Muslims can pray. These prayers often are led by an "imam", who is the leader of the mosque. Shoes must be removed by the worshipers as they enter the mosque prayer room.

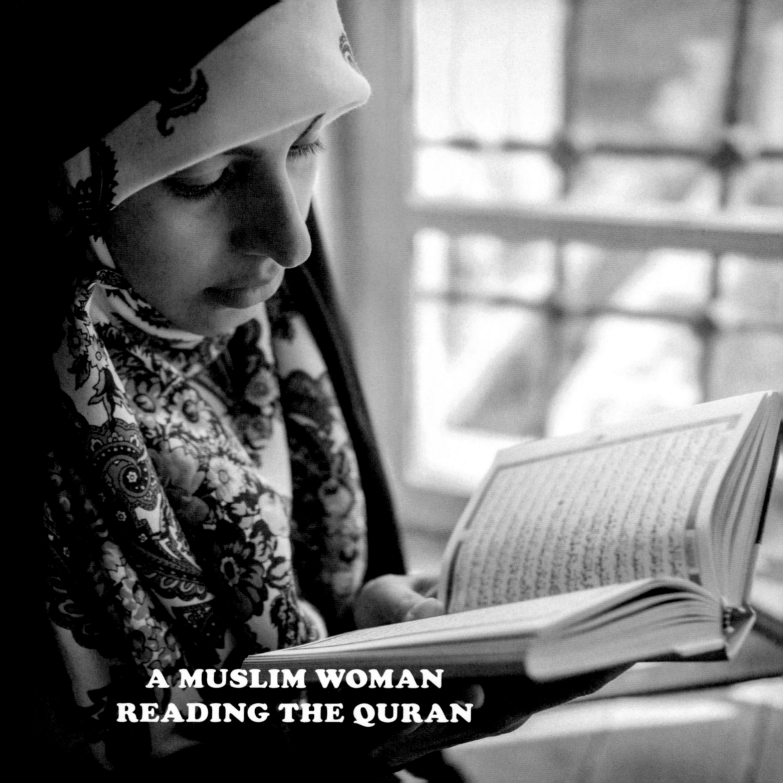

A MUSLIM WOMAN
READING THE QURAN

SHIA AND SUNNI

Like other major religions, there are various sects of Muslims which are groups sharing several similar fundamental beliefs, but do not agree on certain facets of theology. Shia and Sunni are the two biggest groups of Muslims. Approximately 85% of Muslims around the world are Sunni.

BRIEF OVERVIEW OF THE HISTORY OF PAKISTAN

Today, the land that is Pakistan was a part of the Indus Valley civilization from thousands of years before and the civilization had thrived up until 1500 BCE.

BADSHAHI MOSQUE

PAKISTAN

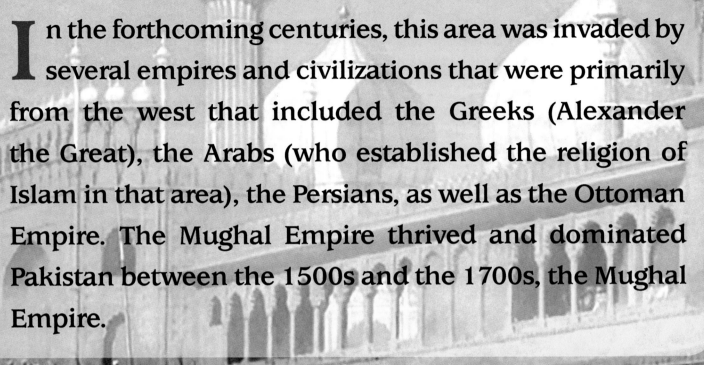

In the forthcoming centuries, this area was invaded by several empires and civilizations that were primarily from the west that included the Greeks (Alexander the Great), the Arabs (who established the religion of Islam in that area), the Persians, as well as the Ottoman Empire. The Mughal Empire thrived and dominated Pakistan between the 1500s and the 1700s, the Mughal Empire.

The British arrived in the region during the 18th century and proceeded to take control of the area of Pakistan, as well as part of India and ruled until 1947. The British split India into three parts in 1947: Pakistan, East Pakistan (which later became Bangladesh), and India. Pakistan and India have always fought over the disputed region known as Kashmir.

Pakistan started testing nuclear weapons in 1998 in response to India performing their own nuclear tests. Relations remain strained between these two countries.

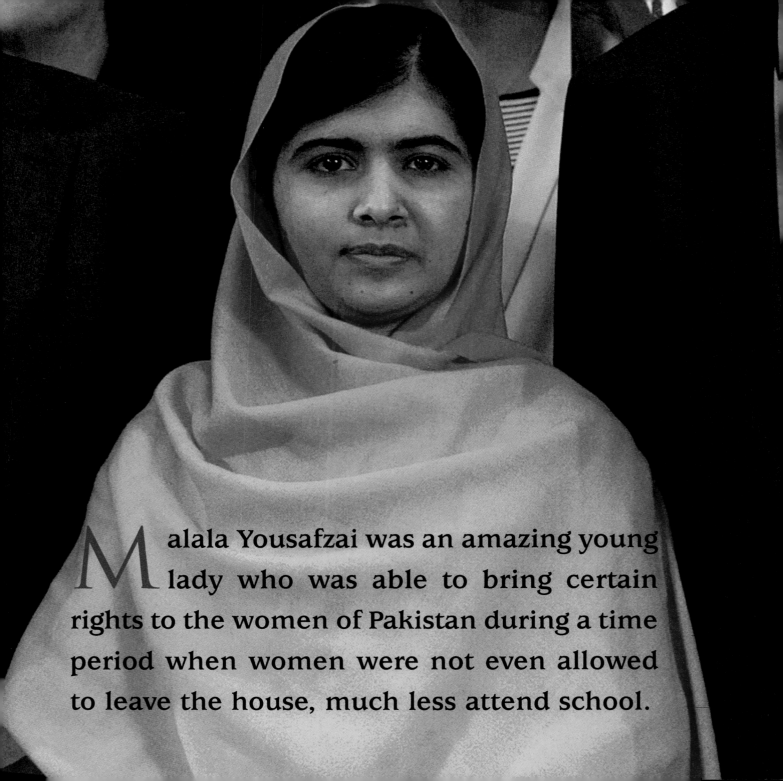

Malala Yousafzai was an amazing young lady who was able to bring certain rights to the women of Pakistan during a time period when women were not even allowed to leave the house, much less attend school.

For additional information, you can go to your local library, research the internet, and ask questions of your teachers, family and friends.

Visit

BABY PROFESSOR
EDUCATION KIDS

www.BabyProfessorBooks.com

to download Free Baby Professor eBooks
and view our catalog of new and exciting
Children's Books

Made in the USA
Monee, IL
16 May 2022

96518791R00040